STO

STO

3-21-72

THE KIBBUTZ

An AMĒCUS STREET Book

THE KIBBUTZ

Life on an Israeli Commune

by Paul J. Deegan

Photographs by Yair Shazar

Editorial Consultation by Yaacov Yisraeli

Research Contributor: Harold Glicken

An AMĒCUS STREET Book

An Imprint of
CREATIVE EDUCATIONAL SOCIETY, INC.
MANKATO, MINNESOTA

An AMECUS STREET Book

PUBLISHED BY CREATIVE EDUCATIONAL SOCIETY, INC.
515 North Front Street, Mankato, Minnesota 56001

Library of Congress Number: 72-156063
Standard Book Number: 87191-053-5

Printed in the United States of America.

Designed by Viking Press, Inc., Minneapolis, Minnesota

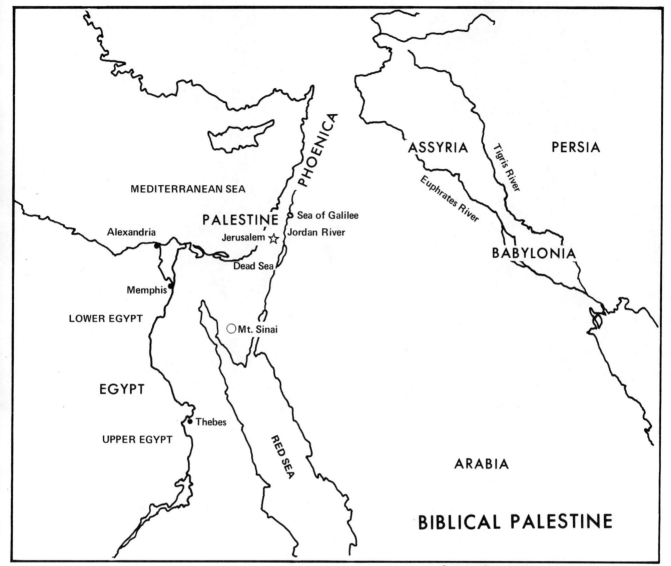

BIBLICAL PALESTINE

In the year 70 A.D. several thousand Jews were completing a year of virtual captivity inside the walled city of Jerusalem. A year before there had been 20,000 of them. But the Romans had surrounded the city and many of them had died from hunger or disease. Those still alive were still intent on defending Jerusalem, the city that had been made the capital of the Land of Israel by King David over 1,000 years before.

But the Roman soldiers under the command of Titus, son of the Roman emperor Vespian, had little trouble overcoming the defenders when the Romans finally crashed the walls. They wrecked the city and set fire to the Second Temple, built in the 6th century B.C. Soon only what is known as the western wall of the Temple Court stood where King Solomon had built the First Temple in about 1,000 B.C.

Jerusalem was conquered. The Temple, center of the then 2,000 year-old Jewish religion — Judaism — was gone.

Nearly 2,000 years later, in the spring of 1948, Jerusalem was again about to be attacked. This time the attackers were Arab soldiers. The attack was coming because for the first time in 1,878 years the Jews were about to again have a nation where they would be self-governing.

On May 14, 1948, a Jewish Provisional Council of State, meeting in Tel Aviv, declared the existence of the State of Israel. The 979-word Proclamation of Independence said in part: ". . . representing the Jewish people in the Land of Israel and the Zionist Movement . . by virtue of our natural and historic right and of the resolution of the General Assembly of the United Nations . . . (we proclaim) the establishment of a Jewish State in the Land of Israel — the State of Israel."

A day later, armies from seven Arab nations attacked the new state. But unlike the results in the first century A.D., the Jews of Israel were not defeated.

The period between the fall of Jerusalem in 70 A.D. and the reestablishment of the State of Israel in 1948 is known as the Diaspora (Die-AS-poh-rah). The word means "scattering" in Greek.

The Jews had been the rulers in Palestine during most of the 600

6

years preceding the Roman victory in Jerusalem. Jewish independence was briefly restored in Judea (the Roman name for Palestine) a few years later. Then came the scattering of the Jews from the Land of Israel. Many were taken to other countries as captives of the many nations or tribes that were to conquer Palestine during the next 1,500 years.

During these centuries there were, at various times, a few thousand to several hundred thousand Jews who remained in the "Promised Land" of the Hebrews, the name by which the Jews of the Old Testament were known.

The rest were scattered throughout the world. Many had settled in the Mediterranean countries until persecutions drove them from Spain and Portugal during the 15th and 16th centuries. Others were in the northern European countries.

Here the word ghetto was first used. It referred to the sections of European cities where Jews were forced to live and where their means of earning a living were restricted by law. In the late 19th century the word pogrom came into use. A pogrom is an organized massacre. The victims in Russia and Poland were the Jews.

A half-century later came the Holocaust, the systematic killing of an estimated six million European Jews by the Nazi government of Germany.

During the Diaspora some Jews had settled in Middle Eastern and North African countries and others had gone to the America's. By 1910 the Jewish population of the United States was the largest of any country in the world. Even today there are more Jews in metropolitan New York than there are in the entire state of Israel.

All through the years of the Diaspora, the Jews, treated as a people apart, had clung to their history and their religion. Both emphasized the idea of returning to Jerusalem, going back to the land where once Jewish kings had ruled in Israel and Judah in central and northern Palestine. The word, "Palestine," was taken from the name of one of the biblical conquerors of the area, the Philistines.

Late in the 19th century a movement, known as Zionism, sprung up among Jews of the Diaspora. This movement activated the long held desire to return to Palestine. The name for the movement comes from Zion, one of the biblical names for Jerusalem, the ancient Holy City of the Jews.

Zionism also gained support because of continued anti-Semitism (visible show of dislike for Jews) in Europe. Zionists began to found settlements in Palestine. The first pioneering village was established in 1878. Four years later the first Aliyah (A-lee-AH, "ascent" in

Hebrew) began. The Aliyah refers to the different groups of Jews who returned or immigrated to Palestine.

The World Zionist Organization was founded in Switzerland in 1898. Its program declared that "The object of Zionism is to establish for the Jewish people a publicly and legally assured home in Palestine." This organization played a leading role in the establishment of the State of Israel. Most of the founders of the state were leaders of the Jewish Agency, the Palestine-based arm of the World Zionist Organization.

When the first Zionists came to Palestine, the area was ruled by the Ottoman Turks. They had conquered the area early in the 16th century. Like the other invaders of Palestine, they took what they could use from the land and then left it in disuse. What had been a healthy agricultural area in biblical days was now mostly a barren wasteland. During the Diaspora, Palestine was usually an unimportant part of a large empire.

The estimated 24,000 Jews living in Palestine prior to the First Aliyah were poor. Most of them lived in the Jewish quarters of the larger cities. They were supported by contributions from Jews of the Diaspora.

But the first groups of Zionists who came to Palestine were men of conviction and desire. Mostly Eastern European Jews, they were generally well-educated and strongly motivated by their ideas. They thought it very important to reclaim the land with their own labor, to work the now-parched soil with their own hands. In Palestine they could again farm the land. They hoped that agriculture would be the principal way of life as it had been thousands of years ago in the first Jewish nations. The Jews had become identified as shopkeepers and merchants during the Diaspora because they were usually not permitted to own land. Sometimes the only livelihood allowed them was that of the peddler.

Determined to erase this pattern of life, most of the pioneer settlers in Palestine were socialists — they believed that the community should own and control the land and what it produced.

One result of their social and political ideas relating to the rebuilding of a Jewish state in Palestine was the kibbutz (kee-BOOTZ).

Kibbutz is the Hebrew word for group.

Hebrew was the language of the biblical Jews and is the language of modern Israel. Hebrew was returned to common use less than a century ago after being used only in religious ceremonies for thousands of years.

A kibbutz is a communal settlement based on the idea that all

members should have equal opportunities, something which had
been denied to almost all Jews of the Diaspora.

The kibbutz economy was based on the Marxist version of
socialism: "From each according to his ability, to each according to
his needs." This principle means that on a kibbutz an orange picker
has the same rights and receives the same benefits as a skilled
engineer. The essential kibbutz practices are group living and common
ownership of property.

Although the kibbutz economy is based on socialism, its government
is democratic. Each member is allowed to vote at the frequent
meetings which determine what takes place on the kibbutz.

Members of a kibbutz are called chaverim (ha-vay-REEM,
"comrade" in Hebrew). The chaverim's theme was: "Here it is good
that we sit together as one." These words make up a lively folk song
that is still popular in Israel.

The first kibbutz was established in 1909 in the swamp-desert of
the Jordan River valley at the southern tip of the Sea of Galilee —
now known as Lake Kinneret (Kee-NER-et, the Hebrew word for
violin which the lake's shape resembles). This kibbutz was called
Deganiah (Deh-GAN-yah, "God's wheat" in Hebrew, the name
given to wild flowers growing in the area).

The founders of the kibbutzim (kee-boo-TZEEM, plural of kibbutz)
were members of the Second Aliyah. This wave of Jews moving to
Palestine made more of an impact that the other Aliyot (A-lee-OT,
plural of Aliyah) on the new Jewish homeland.

The life was difficult for the founders of Deganiah, which is located very close to the 1971 border between Israel and Palestine. It was not easy to make the long-abused land once again fit for farming. And the first kibbutzim were established on the worst land available because this is all that the Arab land-owners would sell to the Jews in Palestine. The land for the kibbutzim was purchased with funds raised by the World Zionist Organization. It was bought as national land by the Jewish National Fund, a Zionist agency.

The Jewish National Fund had provided the 750 acres on which Deganiah was started. Payment was to be one-half of the net profit made from farming the land, soil which had been untouched for years.

The 12 founders of Deganiah had all come to Palestine from Poland. Two of them were women; their average age was 20. They had escaped persecution but had found jobs very scarce in slowly-awakening Palestine. So they had accepted the offer of land and made their own work. And hard work it was. Normal housing and adequate food were also lacking for some time.

One of the founders of Deganiah later married a girl from Russia. One of their children, born after they had left Deganiah, was Moshe Dayan, former commander in chief of the Israeli army and the present Minister of Defense in Israel's cabinet.

The enthusiasm of the kibbutzniks (kee-BOOTZ-niks, those who live on a kibbutz) spread throughout the growing Jewish community. Many who were not attracted by kibbutz life nonetheless identified with the idealism and willingness to work found on kibbutzim. At one time, 12 per cent of the Jewish population in Palestine were kibbutzniks. Many teenagers spent their school vacations working on a kibbutz and the goal of many Jewish youngsters was to become a kibbutznik.

However, the kibbutz life was very different from the life style found in Western countries, even though its principles were rooted in Western thought. The kibbutz was going to attract only a minority of the returned Jews.

But the spark initiated by the chaverim continues to effect life in Israel today. The chaverim were modern Israel's first heroes. This spark did not burn out on the kibbutzim. Today there are over 235 kibbutzim and the nearly 85,000 kibbutzniks make up about 3½ per cent of Israel's 1971 population of 3 million.

Some kibbutzim have fewer than 100 members; others have more than 2,000. They are an important part of Israel's agriculture. Twenty-eight per cent of the country's agricultural products come from the kibbutzim. One-half of Israel's food is supplied by kubbutzim. Kibbutz factories put out 10 per cent of the nation's industrial production. And the influence of kibbutzniks in politics, labor, and the army is much greater than their numbers in relation to the total population.

One-third of the 120-member Knesset (K'NEH-set), Israel's one-house parliament, are past or present kibbutzniks. So are several members of the Cabinet besides Dayan. Two of Israel's five Prime Ministers were once chaverim. They were David Ben-Gurion and Levi Eshkol. Mr. Eshkol died in 1969 but Ben-Gurion, one of the leading figures in the founding of Israel, is still active in national affairs at the age of 84. He lives on a kibbutz in the southern part of Israel.

Ben-Gurion was chosen as the Prime Minister in the first Israeli Cabinet. This was in 1949 after 440,000 of 471,000 Israelis over 18 had voted for a provisional national assembly. The assembly met in the modern part of Jerusalem and became the first Knesset. The same year, Israel was admitted to the United Nations as its 59th member. A year later, the Knesset passed the Law of Return. This legislation gives every Jew anywhere in the world the right to immigrate to Israel.

Ben-Gurion "retired" to his kibbutz in the Negev (NEH-gev) region late in 1952, rejoined the Cabinet as Minister of Defense in February 1955, and in November of that year again became Prime Minister. He resigned in June of 1963.

Many chaverim today have leadership posts in Israel's largest central labor organization, the General Federation of Labor, commonly called Histadrut (His-ta-DROOT, "organization" in Hebrew). Ben-Gurion was one of the founders of Histadrut, which now has one million members, 58 per cent of the adult population of Israel.

Kibbutzniks have also played major roles in the conflict which preceded the establishment of the state and which has continued since 1948. The foes of Jewish self-rule in Palestine were first the Arabs — both those who were living in Palestine and the nations of the Arab world — and, sometimes, the British. Palestine was administered by Great Britain from 1916 until a few hours before the declaration of the State of Israel in 1948. The British governed the region under a 1922 mandate from the League of Nations. This mandate was given to Britain six years after the British army had defeated the Turks in Palestine during World War I.

British withdrawal from the area had been called for in the Partition Plan for Palestine approved by the United Nations General Assembly in November 1947.

The temble hat, worn by many kibbutzniks, looks like an upside-down sailor's hat. The hat, first worn on the kibbutz, became popular throughout the country and became identified with Israelis. Now the hat is bought by tourists and is used by Israeli companies in advertising.

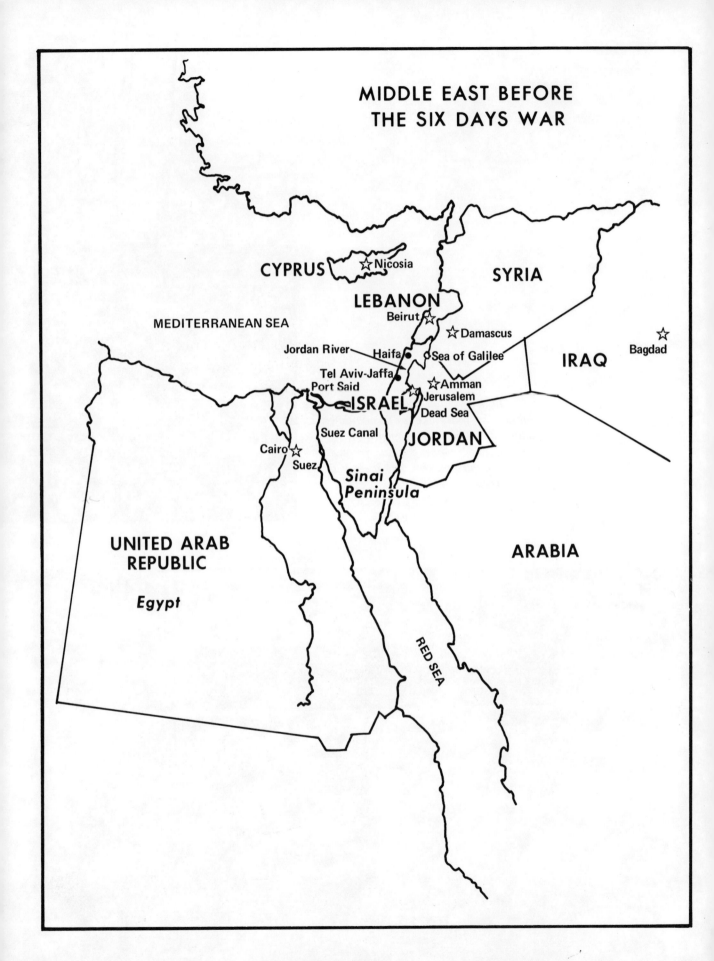

MIDDLE EAST BEFORE
THE SIX DAYS WAR

CYPRUS ☆Nicosia

SYRIA

LEBANON
Beirut☆

☆Damascus

MEDITERRANEAN SEA

Jordan River Haifa● ○Sea of Galilee

Bagdad☆

IRAQ

Tel Aviv-Jaffa●
Port Said
ISRAEL

☆Amman
Jerusalem
Dead Sea

Suez Canal

JORDAN

Cairo☆

Suez

Sinai
Peninsula

UNITED ARAB
REPUBLIC

ARABIA

Egypt

RED SEA

14

The Arab world continued to try to prevent, through military and terrorist actions, the continuance of the Jewish state after it was established. Even in early 1971, the general position of the Arab states is that they do not recognize the existence of the State of Israel.

During the past 23 years, Arab-Israel tensions have resulted in three major military battles — 1948 (known to Israelis as the War of Independence), 1956 (the Sinai Campaign), and 1967 (the Six Days War).

A large percentage of the officers in the Israel Defense Forces — the country's armed services — are kibbutzniks. During the last major Arab-Israeli fighting — the Six Days War — some 200 of the 800 Israeli soldiers killed were kibbutzniks.

The kibbutzim themselves have been and are today part of the Israeli concern with maintaining their existence as a nation. Prior to independence, the kibbutzim were often used as training areas and bases for the Jewish self-defense groups which opposed both Arab terrorists and British officialdom in Palestine. The largest and best organized of these groups was Haganah (Ha-gah-NAH, "defense" in Hebrew), which after independence became the core of the Israel Defense Forces.

Three out of five kibbutzim are located on Israel's borders with the Arab nations of Jordan, Lebanon, and Syria. If these kibbutzim were not there, Israel would have to station part of its small regular army at many more places along the borders than it does now. Some of these border kibbutzim were founded by young Israelis who had been stationed in military outposts at important places along the borders. When their army duty was over, they stayed in these areas, formed kibbutzim, and began developing the land.

Most of the border kibbutzim have watchtowers used to guard against the approach of Arab terrorists. On some kibbutzim, night watchmen patrol the settlement's boundaries, fields are searched each morning for mines, and tractors are armored. There are underground bunkers on many border kibbutzim where young children sleep at night when necessary. When not needed for this purpose, the bunkers are used for playrooms or meeting places.

Kibbutzniks as well as other Israelis believe that they could have accomplished more through the years were it not for the constant concern with defense. Even in June 1971 there were as yet no secure and recognized boundaries in Israel.

The boundaries for the State of Israel when it was established were going to be those described in the UN Partition Plan. This plan took into account the location of the existing kibbutzim in calling for both Jewish and Arab states in Palestine and a new, larger, and internationally-run City of Jerusalem. But the Arabs never acted to establish an Arab state and went to war in an attempt to prevent the survival of the Jewish state. The original UN plans for Palestine are now buried by the military history of the past 23 years.

The present political boundaries in the Middle East (see map on page 18) are the result of cease-fire agreements with the Arab nations following Israel's victory in the 1967 war. The pre-war boundaries of the State of Israel are considered ancient history by most Israelis.

The present state of Israel includes the upper and lower Galilee in the north; the Izrael and Jordan valleys in the north central part of the country; the Mount Carmel area in the center; the 100-mile-long Mediterranean coast line, including the Sharon (SHA-rone) area; the Judean hills inland; and, in the south, the Negev desert and the Aravah (AR-rah-vah) region, a continuation of the Jordan valley which runs south to the Dead Sea.

Most of the West Bank of the Jordan River and the old city of Jerusalem in the east central part of Israel were part of Jordan before the Six Days War.

When the United Arab Republic (Egypt), Syria, and Jordan attacked Israel to touch off the 1967 conflict, Jerusalem was still divided into two hostile cities. Jordan held the old city, the site of places sacred to three religions — Judaism, Christianity, and Islam. The new city on the hills west of the historic Jerusalem was in Israel. The new city was built by Jews during the past 100 years and is the site of Israeli government buildings. It had been made the capital of Israel in 1950.

When the 1967 war ended, the western wall of the Temple Court in the old city was under Jewish control for the first time in 19 centuries. Actually it has been determined that this famous wall was not part of the destroyed Temple, but a retaining wall outside the Temple grounds. But it's still a symbol of Jewish absence from the old city. It is clear today that the Israeli government has no intention of again looking upon a divided Jerusalem.

Besides the West Bank and the old city of Jerusalem, Israeli forces, after the Six Days War, held a narrow 30-mile-long band at the

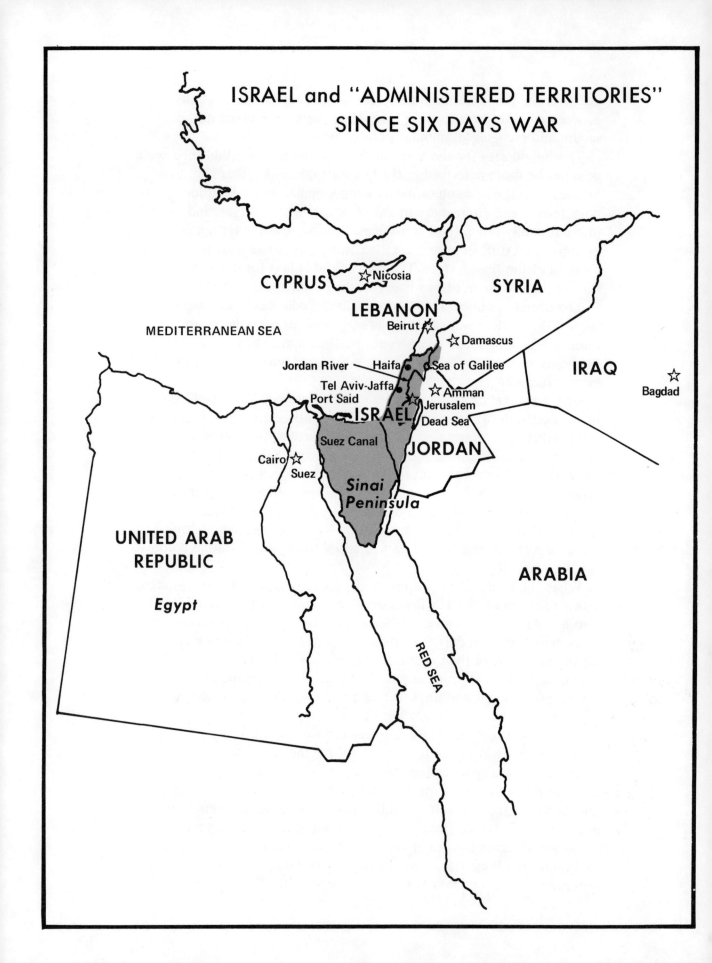

ISRAEL and "ADMINISTERED TERRITORIES" SINCE SIX DAYS WAR

CYPRUS ☆ Nicosia

SYRIA

LEBANON

Beirut ☆

☆ Damascus

MEDITERRANEAN SEA

IRAQ

☆ Bagdad

Jordan River Haifa ● ○ Sea of Galilee

Tel Aviv-Jaffa ●
Port Said

☆ Amman

☆ Jerusalem

ISRAEL

Dead Sea

Suez Canal

JORDAN

Cairo ☆

☆ Suez

Sinai
Peninsula

UNITED ARAB
REPUBLIC

ARABIA

Egypt

RED SEA

south of the Mediterranean coast known as the Gaza Strip, the huge Sinai Peninsula to the southwest of Palestine, and the Golan Heights region northwest of Palestine. Israel has controlled them under the 1967 cease-fire agreements. Israel refers to these areas as "administered territories." This area of 26,500 square miles is more than three times bigger than the pre-war State of Israel. The barren Sinai alone is larger than all of Israel. The Sinai and the Gaza Strip were controlled by the United Arab Republic before 1967. The Golan Heights was part of Syria. Here 12 kibbutzim have been established since 1967.

The forming of permanent political boundaries in the Middle East has been before the United Nations since the passage of a General Assembly resolution in November 1967. This act was to serve as a basis for talks between Arabs and Israel, talks to be directed at achieving a permanent settlement and a lasting peace in the Middle East.

Attempts to accomplish these goals through bargaining were still being made in the spring of 1971. The governments of the United Arab Republic and Jordan had recently indicated that they would admit the existence of the State of Israel; the Israelis were considered by most observers to be willing to withdraw from most of the Sinai, part of the West Bank, and part of the Golan Heights. The Israelis say that they must retain some of these areas in order to maintain secure borders in the future. Despite some changes in positions of both Arabs and Israelis, there was no clear indication in June 1971 that a settlement was soon to be reached.

Israel, minus the administered territories, is a very small nation of only 7,993 square miles, about the size of the state of New Jersey. It is less than 45 miles from east to west at its widest point; it is only 260 miles from the northeast corner to the southeast edge of the Negev.

There are four times more Jews in Israel today — 2.6 million — than there were when independence was declared — 650,000. A little over 8 per cent of them live in the now unified Jerusalem. The total Jewish population of Israel is now 10 times the number of Jews who were in Palestine at the time of the First Aliyah.

Yet the number of Jews in the United States today — some 5.4 million — is more than twice the number in Israel. Over 17,000 Jews have moved to Israel from the United States since the Six Days War. This is twice as many as had come to Israel in the previous 20 years. There are also nearly a million more Jews in the Soviet Union today — an estimated 3.5 million ("officially" only 2.1 million) — than there are in Israel.

Israel's total 1971 population of 3 million includes over 400,000 non-Jews, most of whom are Arabs. Many of them are Palestinian Arabs who fled in 1948 but returned after the first Arab-Israeli war. There are three times as many Arabs in the State of Israel today as there were in 1948.

Another 990,000 Arabs live in the areas now being administered by Israel and over 200,000 of them live in refugee camps. The status of these refugees is one of the problem items in reaching a Middle East peace settlement. These refugees are also a constant reminder that Israel is a new nation in an ancient region; a Western-style state amid a Middle-Eastern culture.

Most of the Arabs who are citizens of Israel live in the cities or larger towns. Over 70,000 are residents of Jerusalem. Nazareth, the historical home of Jesus, is an Arab town of some 32,000 persons. Over 80 percent of the Arab population of Israel votes in Israel's elections. More than one-half of the Arab workers belong to Histadrut. Arabic as well as Hebrew is an official language in Israel and the schools in Arab communities use Arabic.

Many Western ways — including a democratic government — were brought to Israel by the first Jewish immigrants. Yet the younger Israeli, who has known no other homeland, is attracted by the Arab-dominated Middle Eastern culture. He likes many of the Arab customs. He considers himself a Middle Easterner, not a European nor an American.

So there is a growing bond between the young Israeli and the millions of Arabs that live around him, despite the longstanding and bitter conflict between Jews and both Arab nations and Palestinian Arabs. The young man or woman born in Israel does not hate the Arabs but rejects the positions toward Israel taken by Arab leaders.

The young Israeli is determined to live in peace with his Arab neighbors. He wants to adopt what he sees as good in their life-style. He hopes to be able to share with them his more advanced educational system and his Western-based approach to making a living and using the land. Peace, this Israeli believes, will also enable him to carry forward his nation's efforts to restore an ancient heritage in a long empty and wasted land.

Not surprisingly then, the usual greeting and farewell on a kibbutz — and throughout Israel — is shalom (sha-LOM, "peace" in Hebrew).

The chaverim still hope for peace in the Middle East even though military conflict or the threat of attack has been part of the life of almost all past and present kibbutzniks. Chaverim believe that they will not be able to live the kibbutz way to its fullest until peace comes, relieving the pressures produced by a lack of security.

On kibbutzim, grandchildren of the original kibbutzniks are now coming into leadership roles. They are in a position to follow, while trying to advance and enrich, a pattern of living that has been developed over the past 60 years. There have already been some changes.

Large industrial operations have been developed on many kibbutzim although agriculture remains an important part of kibbutz life. Machinery is commonly used in the fields and in the factories, replacing to some extent the manual labor so highly valued by the founders of the kibbutzim. The early kibbutzniks would not hire workers from outside the kibbutzim. They wanted to do all the work on the kibbutz themselves. This practice is no longer so strict because some kibbutzim need more manpower than is available on a kibbutz. However, the principle is still highly respected.

Neither are today's kibbutzniks held to their way of life by the idealism that marked the first kibbutzniks. The younger chaverim have heard the criticism that their life style is an escape from reality. But they do not agree. Instead they see life on the kibbutz as both productive for themselves and the country and personally rewarding.

Israel authors Herbert Russcol and Margalit Banai, writing in the book, The First Million Sabras, reflect on the kibbutzim as follows:

"The kibbutzim gave Israel its unique character as a social experiment. They are a national heritage of gallant men and women who were not afraid to dream of the Good Place where man would live with his brother in brotherhood. With all their shortcomings, they are the most admirable, the most successful, voluntary socialism since the communes of early Christians in the earlier centuries after Christ."

This book shows and tells about life on modern kibbutzim, the communal settlements of Israel. Although each kibbutz differs slightly in its daily operations, the life-style on kibbutzim is very similar. The intent of this book is to show typical kibbutz activities and not the exact way of life on a specific kibbutz.

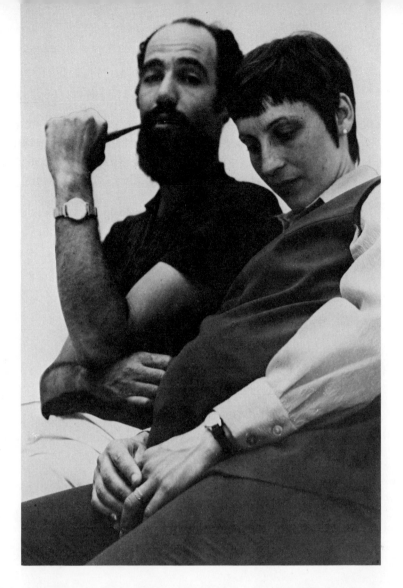

Group living on most kibbutzim begins at birth. Native born Israelis are called sabras (SAH-bras, "cactus" in Hebrew). The cactus plant is tough on the outside, sweet on the inside. Sabras are seen as possessing similar characteristics. Many of these qualities are said to be rooted in kibbutz life. The unique kibbutz approach to raising children has established many of these qualities.

The woman on a kibbutz has always been considered an equal of the man; her primary relationship was to the group which guaranteed her support. The first kibbutzniks did not want to weaken this relationship and when children were born on the kibbutz, the chaverim were forced to find a way of keeping the woman's role intact. She would have to be able to work at jobs important to the whole community, rather than concentrate exclusively on her family.

This outlook led to the concept of Children's Houses. The babies would grow up in their own group living situations — a kibbutz within a kibbutz.

A few days after birth, a kibbutz baby is placed in a nursery where a specially trained nurse-teacher, called a metapelet (meh-tah-PEL-et — plural, metaplot: meh-tah-P'LOT, nouns formed from the Hebrew verb meaning "to take care"), is in charge. A mother, ema (EE-mah) in Hebrew, nurses her baby with other new mothers. The mother or father — aba (AH-ba) in Hebrew — may visit their baby in the nursery at any time.

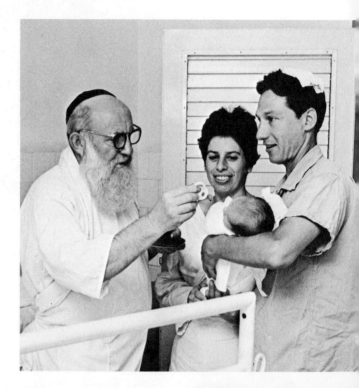

The circumcision of male infants is a Jewish religious tradition dating back to Abraham. The Bible records that God made an agreement with Abraham, telling him that his offspring would become a great nation. God told Abraham that the males should be circumcised as a sign of the agreement or covenant. The circumcision takes place eight days after birth, the time given Abraham by God. It is performed by a religious leader known as a mohel (mo-HEL).

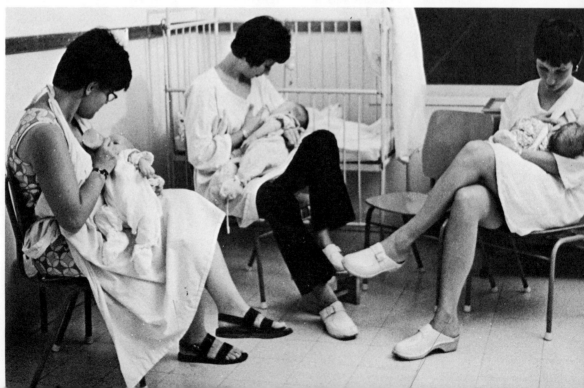

As the infant gets older, he will be with his parents for a couple of hours late in the afternoon, through the early evening hours. The family is also together on the weekend and on holidays. Most parents also take a few minutes during the day to spend with their young children.

Though the mother may bathe her baby and frequently put him to bed, the children's houses are run by the metaplot. A metapelet determines the child's diet, his toilet training, and is responsible for other things such as discipline, usually left in the hands of the parents.

After a year spent in the nursery, children live in a Toddlers' House until they are four years old. On a few kibbutzim, Deganiah included, children spend the night with their parents.

The two to four-year olds learn many of the characteristics identified with the sabra, both on and off the kibbutz. Two of the most noticeable are self-reliance and a strong friendship between, as well as a sense of responsibility for, other children of his age.

Observers of kibbutz children note that they seldom quarrel and fight with one another. The metaplot stress the importance of sharing play things because a principle of kibbutz life is that there is no private property. During these early years, the children eat together and share some of the work of keeping their dormitories clean and orderly.

Most kibbutz children from five to seven years old live in dormitories in groups of three or four. They attend a grade school known as beit seifer (bet SEH-fer) where they are introduced to new metaplot and new teachers. They also become members of a children's society, called Chevrat Yeladim (Hev-RAT Ye-la-DEEM).

The society introduces them to the basics of kibbutz living. The children govern themselves, making their decisions at group meetings. An elected officer, usually a sixth-grader, presides at these meetings. All of the children have an equal vote. All the things used in the beit sefer are collectively owned.

Each child receives an allowance of several lirot (lee-ROTE, Israeli money — 3½ lirot equals one U. S. dollar) a year to spend as he wants. The child's clothes, food, books, medical care, and other necessities are provided through the beit sefer by the kibbutz.

The children in beit sefer have their own small farm. This gives them an opportunity to become acquainted with work on the kibbutz. They sell their farm products, perhaps oranges, vegetables, and chickens, to the kibbutz. The money received goes into a special fund. Its use is determined by a vote of the group. It might be used for field trips, new playground equipment, or a phonograph.

School work in the beit sefer begins at 6:30 a.m. and continues until about noon. Breaks are taken for breakfast and a mid-morning snack. Afternoon projects help the students to become familiar with their kibbutz surroundings, such as the animals and flowers. Afternoons are also spent hiking, preparing holiday programs, and studying history, architecture, and music. Beit sefer children work from 30 to 60 minutes a day on their part of the kibbutz and also help in the dormitory with such activities as setting the table for meals and cleaning up after meals.

After chores and a rest period, the children visit their parents, who live nearby. The time at which children go to see their parents differs from kibbutz to kibbutz but it is usually late in the afternoon. The early evening hours are reserved for family activities only. Parents and children are together without interruption. Sometimes the parents play with a child or a family might walk, talk, or read.

Saturday or Shabbat (shah-BAAT, "to stop (work)" in Hebrew) is a day kibbutzniks spend doing things as a family.

Shabbat is observed throughout Israel as a day of rest. On the kibbutz and elsewhere in the country, people work a six-day week. Saturday is the "weekend." Work stops a couple of hours earlier than usual on Friday because Shabbat begins at sundown on Friday and continues until nightfall on Saturday. Shabbat is a day for worship among religious Jews, who also limit their activities during the 24-hour period.

The work week resumes on Sunday morning in Israel. During the week, the children will spend most of the daytime hours with those of their own age and the metaplot.

The relationship between child and parents on a kibbutz is more like that between a young person and older, trusted friends than it is to the usual child-parent relationship. Perhaps the fact that parents are not primarily responsible for disciplining their young children — parental spankings are very rare on the kibbutz — is the principal reason for that type of relationship. The child might also feel more free with his parents because, unlike children brought up in most Western families, he is not particularly dependent upon them.

Children leave the beit seifer at age 12 for junior-senior high school. Often several kibbutzim will join to build a regional school. This school for 7th through 12th graders is called a mosad (mo-SAAD). The students will stay in dormitories at the mosad during the week if it is not located on their kibbutz. They will be bussed home for Shabbat and maybe one other night during the week, holidays, and summer vacation.

The mosad also has a small farm. Students here have livestock and poultry operations. The teenagers continue to work in different areas of the kibbutz and some discover areas of personal interest. The mosad farm's products are sold to the kibbutzim. The money is spent for things of interest to the students.

Classes on the mosad begin at 6:45 a.m. and continue until 12:30 p.m. Time is taken for breakfast and a mid-morning break. Courses include art, humanities, languages, math, music, science courses, and social studies. The sciences studied include biology, chemistry, and physics. The languages offered are usually English, French, and Arabic. Vocational courses are also taught. These include agricultural subjects, electronics, mechanics, and sewing.

Following lunch, the main meal of the day throughout Israel, the students work for several hours at tasks on their mosad. If the mosad is located on their parents' kibbutz, the students may visit with their families until dinner. If the students are living away from their kibbutz, the time between work and dinner is a free period.

After dinner come sports events, club meetings, and time for homework. Kibbutz teenagers do not date "American-style." All activities are for the group and everyone is expected to participate.

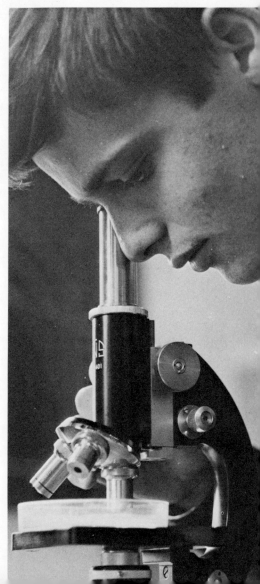

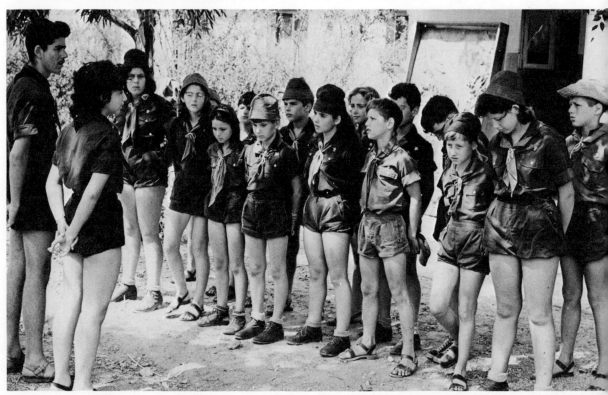

The whole mosad meets once each week. An elected officer, usually
a high school senior, chairs the meeting. A central committee
coordinates most of the social and technical problems of the mosad,
including work assignments and student complaints. Other
committees schedule athletics, care for the library, and plan social
functions. These can include camping, dances, field trips into the
desert regions, forestry, hiking, and scouting. There are also cultural
committees dealing with activities such as the mosad orchestra. Club
activities might include art, chess, dramatics, folk dancing, literature,
or politics.

Adults are present on the mosad as teachers, nurses, musicians, and agricultural advisers from the kibbutzim. The general atmosphere of the mosad is informal and the relationship of the adults with the junior-senior high school students is open and casual. Dress is informal in the mosad and children call adults by their first names. Although the adults serve as advisers, even functions such as disciplining students are handled by a committee of students.

Upon graduating from the mosad, both boys and girls must serve in the Israel Defense Forces. Boys now serve for three years, women for 20 months. Women fill non-fighting roles, freeing more men to carry arms. Officers in Israel's armed forces are generally younger than in other Western countries. Many of the officers are from kibbutzim. Many of the pilots in Israel's air force, regarded by other nations as one of the world's best, are kibbutzniks. The kibbutz training in group living and discipline make kibbutzniks well-regarded soldiers. They, like all Israelis, also feel a deep responsibility to serve their country.

The Israel Defense Forces are very dependent on reservists — men and women who have completed their regular tour of duty. Because the nation is small, Israeli leaders decided the country could not support a large standing army. Instead the regular army depends on a very large number of reservists. Men remain in the reserves until they are 55. Until they are 40, they train for at least one full month of each year. Women who have no children remain in the reserves until they are 34.

Kibbutz youth finishing their army duty might want to spend a year on a kibbutz other than their own, especially a newer one along the border. Then they often will return to their own kibbutz where after a year's trial period they may become full members.

Membership in a kibbutz brings the right to vote at the weekly meetings. Membership, even on the kibbutz where one is born, is considered a privilege, not a right. Young persons returning to the kibbutz from army service live in private rooms. They receive the same benefits as their parents. They can begin a vocation on the kibbutz.

Some young kibbutz members decide to leave their kibbutz and live and work in a city, rather than starting in a job on the kibbutz. They might go to Tel Aviv, Israel's largest city with a population of 385,000.

The kibbutz also encourages its young people to seek specialized education. Some are sent to teachers' training colleges so they can become qualified to teach at a mosad. Others study art or drama so they can teach these subjects on the kibbutz. Still others attend universities or institutes to study agricultural or technical subjects which can be useful on their kibbutz.

Most of the youngsters raised on a kibbutz find the life attractive. Four out of five of them become members of a kibbutz. But the kibbutz does not attract the percentage of new immigrants that it did earlier in this century. The population of Israel more than doubled from 1948 to 1967 as one million immigrants came to live in the new state. Most of these newcomers came from Mediterranean and North African countries and were not familiar with the traditions of the kibbutz; nor were they attracted by the Western-based kibbutz philosophies.

The young kibbutz members, though, apparently believe that the kibbutz is where their lives can be spent in the most worthwhile manner. They will work at farming, in the many factories now found on kibbutzim, or do specialized work such as teaching.

A kibbutz can be described as a cooperative village where hundreds of people work together. It differs from another type of agricultural village found in Israel — the moshav (mo-SHAV). In the moshav, each family works an allotted plot of land. The products are combined for marketing; equipment is purchased on a group basis. But each family on the moshav retains an income for itself. Children on the moshav live with their parents.

On a kibbutz all profits are turned back into the kibbutz treasury for the benefit of all chaverim and the growth of the settlement. There is not much private property on kibbzutzim, although chaverim often receive small gifts from non-kibbutzniks.

Both the kibbutz and the moshav are almost always located on government-owned land. One of the basic principles of Zionism was that the land in the Jewish state was to remain nationally-held. This policy was adopted to prevent hoarding of land and individual profit-taking by individuals who might hold the land for future sale, a practice that would also slow land development. Thus 92 per cent of the land in Israel is owned by the state. The land is leased to a kibbutz or a moshav for 49-year periods which may be renewed.

Today most of the land in Israel that can be profitably farmed is already settled. The land used by kibbutzim is regarded by government officials as being especially well-used. And kibbutzniks have long been recognized as hard workers. Each member knows that his failure to work will hurt the kibbutz and, therefore, himself.

Perhaps because of this attitude, there are no policemen or jails on the kibbutz. Chaverim actually police themselves and thefts or any kind of crime are very rare on the kibbutz. The fact that kibbutzniks have few material needs is another factor in the absence of crime. The kibbutz assumes responsibility for providing things people need. These services include the presence of medical doctors and dentists and the assurance of care in old age.

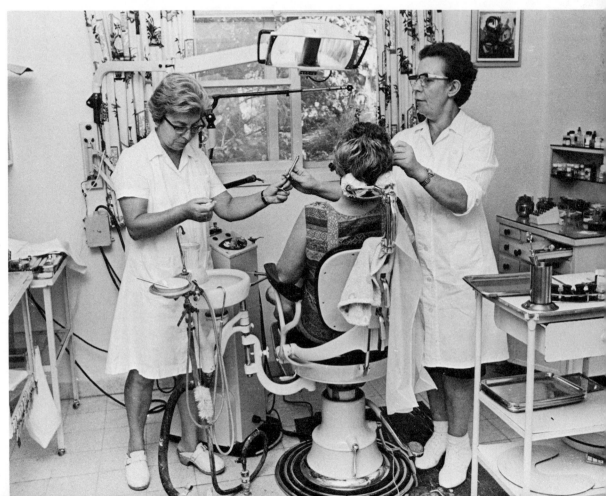

The kibbutz way of life has attracted Jews from all over the world. Jews now living in Israel have come there from over 100 other nations.

The democratic political structure of the kibbutzim is centered around the General Assembly. This includes all members of a kibbutz. Each member has a vote in all decisions made at weekly meetings. These meetings are usually held on Saturday night in the dining hall, which is the center of the kibbutz. Lively debate takes place and everyone is free to express his opinions at these meetings. All opinions must be heard before a decision affecting chaverim is made.

The General Assembly elects officers for a kibbutz, approves new members, and decides on the kibbutz budget. Other kibbutz government personnel are also chosen by the assembly. There are committees dealing with members' needs, such as housing, cultural activities, and education. The heads of various kibbutz departments, such as the orchards or the factory, are also elected.

The most important government post on the kibbutz is the General Secretary. He is part of the Secretariat which might also include the treasurer and important department heads such as farm manager, factory manager, labor coordinator, and education director.

Kibbutz officials receive the same benefits as workers — they get nothing extra. On smaller kibbutzim, these officials perform their administrative tasks in addition to working a full day at a regular kibbutz job. These elected officials serve from six months to two years. The kibbutz changes its leaders often, following the principle of equality. The committes that work with the kibbutz officials are also elected. Neither the executives nor the committee members receive payment for their work.

The efforts of the kibbutz labor coordinator are extremely important. This man or woman must assign chaverim to work posts each day. Most kibbutzniks have special skills or training and work at the same jobs each day. This would be true of a technician in a factory. But others, including some who are well-educated, go from job to job on the kibbutz.

The various department heads approach the labor coordinator each evening and either ask for more workers for the following day or tell him that they have finished a project and will need less help. The labor coordinator and the department head work out compromises to supply enough men to satisfy most of the requests.

This task is carried out by personal contact, not by writing memos. Most business communication is taken care of in this manner on the kibbutz. Direct contact saves time and permits decisions to be made without paperwork. There are few memos passing around a kibbutz.

After the labor coordinator makes his work assignments for the following day, he posts the list in the dining hall. He does this before the evening meal.

It's the labor coordinator's job to see that the most important jobs are done first. When the foreman of the citrus groves tells him that more workers are needed to pick oranges, which will soon rot if not picked, the labor coordinator must find the manpower without hurting production in another critical area. The greenhouse foreman might object to losing his help for a week if the rose bushes need to be pruned. But if the pruning can wait, he'll agree to let his regular help pick oranges. He knows that next week he might be able to get more help than usual in order to make up the lost time.

The kibbutz founders, it's been noted, frowned on hiring outside help. They felt that it was wrong to use other people in order to gain a profit for themselves. However, many kibbutzim now hire temporary workers.

Both work which is productive (money-making) and work which is service are necessary on the kibbutz. Service jobs include food preparation, cooking, and serving; caring for children; teaching; and washing clothes. These functions are vital to the daily lives of most of us, including kibbutzniks. There is little heavy work necessary in many of the service jobs. Therefore, they are generally done by women.

Other service jobs, such as those in the carpentry shops and those related to the upkeep of the kibbutz buildings and property, are done mostly by men.

A kibbutz also needs products to sell so that it will have money to continue in existence and, hopefully, to grow. The productive work areas include agricultural operations, such as growing cotton or fruit or taking care of livestock, and manufacturing plants. Work in the productive areas of a kibbutz is similar to work in any large, modern farm or factory in the United States. Men drive tractors, combines, or trucks; some climb ladders to pick fruit; others operate machines in factories.

A woman may choose to work in the productive areas of the kibbutz but men do most of this type of work. The chicken houses and some factories are exceptions — many women work there.

Chaverim in a service job such as a laundry might iron shirts all day. This can be boring work; so are some other necessary kibbutz jobs. A chaver (HA-ver, singular of chaverim) may ask the labor coordinator for a different job. If other work is available and someone else is willing to iron shirts, the laundry worker can be transferred to a job he likes better. The labor coordinator tries to give each chaver a job he wants.

Sometimes, however, a chaver must work at a job he dislikes. He tries to do this without complaining if the job is essential and he can do it well. Other kibbutzniks don't look down on him because all jobs on the kibbutz have equal status. Chaverim working at boring tasks try to keep up interesting conversations with their co-workers and they usually have a radio on. They work with the thought that they are contributing something to the kibbutz and thus to themselves.

Most kibbutzniks work an eight-hour day, six days a week. So do most Israelis living in urban areas.

Teachers, nurses, and other professionals usually also work at physical jobs, such as picking oranges, for a certain number of days each year. This helps to retain the emphasis on physical work, a principle on which the kibbutzim were founded. Those chaverim who usually perform physical tasks also take turns at serving food or watching the children in the dormitories at night.

It is not common, but some kibbutzniks who have a profession work outside of the kibbutz. The kibbutz provides them with transportation to their jobs in the city. Like the other chaverim, they too are provided with clothing and their other expenses are paid for by the kibbutz. These chaverim in turn give their salaries to the kibbutz.

The chaver teaching at a university in the city or serving in the government or other national offices must still perform some duties on the kibbutz. Members of the Knesset, for example, can be found washing dishes in the kitchen when they return to their kibbutz on the weekend.

Most of the chaverim working in the productive areas are involved in agriculture. The crops a kibbutz raises depend on its location. Even in this small nation temperature and climate differs. The Judean hills, lower Galilee, and the coastal plain have warm temperatures, which fall to the upper 40's at night in the winter months, and moderate rainfall. Some of the inland valleys and the Negev have very hot weather and little rainfall.

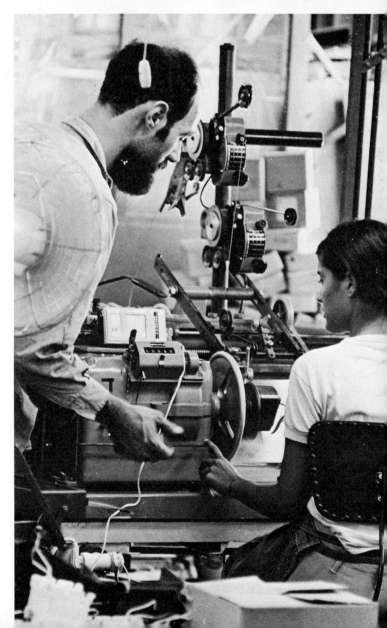

Citrus fruits are common crops in many areas north of the Negev. These might be grapefruit, lemons, oranges, or tangerines. But kibbutzim also grow apples, artichokes, bananas, cotton, olives, peanuts, potatoes, tomatoes, and walnuts. Some kibbutzim raise fish — usually carp — either in natural waters or in artificial ponds.

Crops are planted under the supervision of kibbutz experts. Some have studied at agricultural colleges in the United States. They make sure that proper irrigation — a necessity in many parts of Israel — is followed and that the right insecticides (chemicals used to control insects) are used. Planting follows a pattern that ensures a continual harvest. Citrus fruits, for example, begin to ripen in November on some kibbutzim and picking continues into spring. Then potatoes are planted. When this job is done, there's cotton to irrigate. The idea is not to have projects, each requiring many workers, taking place at the same time.

Some kibbutzim grow flowers as a product. Flowers are started in greenhouses, picked when in bloom, and usually exported (sent out of the country) for sale. Flowers from kibbutz greenhouses are sometimes sent by airplane to Europe or the United States where they might be on sale 24 hours after being picked.

Livestock and poultry are also important to the economy of many kibbutzim. Herds of cattle are sent out to pasture by modern cowboys, who often substitute a jeep or a tractor for a horse. But horses are more important in some kibbutz livestock operations than they are today in the United States. The youngsters on the kibbutz like to play among the "kibbutz cowboys."

Sheep are raised on kibbutzim and teenage girls sometimes help take care of them. Sheep are raised both for meat and for wool.

Large dairy operations are common on kibbutzim. Automated milking, separating, and pasteurizing equipment are found in the dairy barns. Alongside the modern equipment, chaverim engage in one of the unpopular jobs on the kibbutz, keeping the milking areas spotless.

Poultry are found on most kibbutzim. Some raise turkeys but chickens are more common. The sale of chicken eggs for food and to hatcheries is also a big business. Women work at many of the jobs in the chicken houses. These buildings often have central heating and air conditioning to ensure top production. Modern equipment is also used in feeding the poultry.

The sale of food in Israel is governed by the dietary laws of Judaism. These laws specify the way animals must be killed and prepared. They also forbid the eating of some foods such as pork. Combinations of other foods, such as meat and milk, are also forbidden. The dietary laws are not closely observed on most kibbutzim nor by many other Israeli Jews. It is estimated that only 20 per cent of the Jews in Israel seriously practice Orthodox Judaism. However, all food prepared for sale must meet the religious regulations.

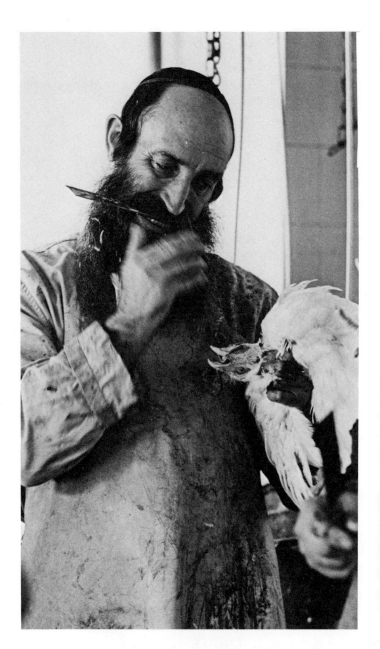 

Kibbutzim also raise barley, cotton, sorghum, sunflowers, and wheat. Extensive irrigation is necessary in some cases. Modern machinery, some of it purchased in Europe or the United States, is used for preparing the soil, planting, cultivating, and harvesting.

The kibbutz economy was once identified only with agriculture. Industry has become a major factor within the past 15 years. Up to one-half of all kibbutz income now comes from manufacturing. The lack of productive land was one factor in the move to industrial operations. The change also offered employment to more kibbutzniks.

There are some 175 factories on kibbutzim. They manufacture or assemble a variety of products. These include electrical parts, irrigation equipment, plastics, plywood, potash, precision-tooled screws, and textiles. There are also canning factories.

Some factories were built primarily to provide jobs for older chaverim. The kibbutz tries to provide older members with jobs which can be important to the kibbutz. This is one way the kibbutz fulfills its goals of taking care of all its members and treating all alike.

The productive areas of the kibbutz are marked by the use of the most modern equipment and the latest techniques. Supervisors are often sent abroad for specialized education. When new heavy equipment is purchased, a kibbutz frequently sends the man who will operate it to the factory in Europe or the United States for training.

Manual labor was a trademark of the first kibbutzniks and a good deal of it is still needed on today's kibbutzim. But the amount of labor available is limited — on the kibbutz and throughout the relatively small population of Israel. If Israeli products are to bring a profit on the world market, they must be produced in the most efficient way possible.

Assistance in agriculture and manufacturing is available to the kibbutz from national organizations of kibbutzim.

Each kibbutz is a member of a federation. There are four major movements or federations of kibbutzim. They are based on social and political philosophies. The three larger federations each represent between 25,000 and 30,000 chaverim. And all the federations have representation in the Kibbutz Movement Alliance.

Each federation has modern offices in cities such as Tel Aviv. Here there are data-processing equipment, technicians, and experts in all phases of kibbutz life, all available to member kibbutzim. The federations also offer financial help. Their technical advice includes farm management courses.

These federations have also set up concerns similar in some ways to United States farm cooperatives. Kibbutzim can thus make use of central purchasing services. They can obtain the use of heavy machinery — bulldozers or combines for example — when needed. Construction crews are available from these concerns to put up large buildings. Local chaverim will often assist with the finishing work, such as painting, in order to keep alive the kibbutz tradition of self-reliance. Kibbutzim distribute some of their products through federation-owned regional packing and freezing centers.

Food concentrates for animals are an example of the items purchased by the kibbutz through a federation. The feed is delivered to kibbutzim in federation-owned trucks, specially equipped for unloading the product. Federation milk trucks also make regular stops at kibbutz dairy barns.

Kibbutz products are sold both in Israel and in nations throughout the world. Some products are sold directly by the kibbutz. Others are sold through Tnuva (T'noo-VAH), a Histadrut agency which is a national agricultural marketing cooperative.

The work force on kibbutzim usually includes some non-Israelis known as volunteers. Kibbutzim offer people from all countries and all religions the opportunity to volunteer their work in exchange for food, clothing, and lodging.

There is a special program for volunteers on many kibbutzim. They are known as ulpanim (ul-pan-EEM). This is also the name for "crash" courses in Hebrew given throughout Israel to newcomers. The kibbutz volunteers spend half of each day studying Hebrew and several hours working on the kibbutz. The programs last from one to six months. Volunteers who complete the six-month program often have a good knowledge of Hebrew. They also know quite a lot about the kibbutz way of life. The kibbutzim sponsor trips throughout Israel for volunteers in these programs.

The volunteers receive most of the benefits given to chaverim although they cannot vote at the general meetings. They work at the same jobs assigned to chaverim — taking care of cattle, poultry or sheep; picking fruit; or working in the factories, fish ponds, kitchen, or laundry. Some work, such as teaching or caring for children, is usually done only by chaverim.

While kibbutzniks find their life stimulating and rewarding, daily life on a kibbutz is not particularly exciting. A chaver is usually up at dawn and in the field by 6 a.m. — earlier in the hot summer months. Breakfast is served at 8 a.m. Food is served family style in the dining hall. The food is brought from the kitchen on heated carts. Breakfast consists of porridge, eggs, herrings, vegetables, yogurt (a thick custard-like fermented drink made from milk), tea, and coffee.

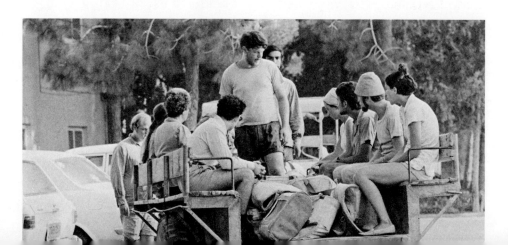

After breakfast the chaverim go back into the fields or to other jobs for the rest of the morning. There is a constant exchange of talk on the kibbutz during the day. Subjects include politics, the kibbutz, social events, and children. The mid-morning coffee break is a kibbutz institution. Radios can be found in most places of work. Field workers bring transistor radios with them. The hourly news broadcasts are important because they provide information on the latest in Israeli-Arab relations. Each hour, on the hour, workers listen carefully to the news.

At noon chaverim return to the kibbutz dining hall to eat what in Israel is the main meal of the day. On the kibbutzim, lunch consists of soup, vegetables, meat, potatoes, fruit, and coffee. After this meal, chaverim often discuss problems with the labor coordinator.

On most days, chaverim return to their living quarters at 3:30 p.m. to shower and change clothes. Children come to see their parents at 4 p.m. and the next few hours are spent in family activities.

Dinner is served at 7 p.m. and is similar to breakfast.

Kibbutzniks receive food, clothing and shelter from the kibbutz. Clothing is supplied, washed, mended, and ironed by kibbutz workers. Chaverim deposit their dirty clothes at the laundry on Sunday. They pick up clean and mended clothing in their assigned bins on the following Friday.

Some kibbutzim have tailors who make Shabbat clothes. Others allow chaverim a small allowance and they purchase Shabbat clothes in the city.

Each kibbutz has a store where such items as candy, coffee, and gifts can be obtained. Members may have a certain amount of these things. However, such items as soap, razor blades, and cigarets are provided whenever a chaver needs them. There is no private property on the kibbutz except for these small items.

Adults on most established kibbutzim live in small apartments. These have often been built by kibbutz members. A living room, bedroom, and bathroom are usually the only rooms in the apartment. Most apartments are tastefully decorated. Furniture belongs to the kibbutz and is distributed according to seniority — the longer a member has been in a kibbutz, the better his furniture. Seniority, along with equality, is a basic kibbutz principal. Some kibbutzim are installing air conditioning in their apartments — summer temperatures regularly reach the high 90's in some parts of Israel.

A television set would be very unusual in a kibbutz apartment. Israel does not have widespread television programing. Radios, newspapers, and conversation are the primary sources of news and communication on kibbutzim.

Newspapers are well read in Israel. Since the country is small, papers printed in the cities can be quickly delivered throughout the nation. There are 21 morning and two afternoon daily papers. Thirteen of them are in Hebrew; some are affiliated with political parties and two are backed by Histadrut. The other 10 dailies are printed in several languages, including English, German, Polish, Arabic, and Yiddish (a language developed during the Diaspora by Eastern European Jews).

Many chaverim plant gardens and grow flowers outside of their apartments. They do this during their leisure time. A good deal of time is spent in the apartment yards when the weather is pleasant.

The apartments have only very small kitchens where snacks can be prepared. All meals are eaten in the communal dining hall. The dining hall is the heart of the kibbutz. It is also used for meetings and other group activities or entertainment, such as movies. The dining hall is often the nicest — and busiest — building on the kibbutz. Many people linger here after the evening meal to exchange news of the day or plan a trip for the weekend.

The various youth movements among kibbutzim also bring a young man or woman together with the person he or she will later marry. Young kibbutzniks seldom marry someone from their own kibbutz,

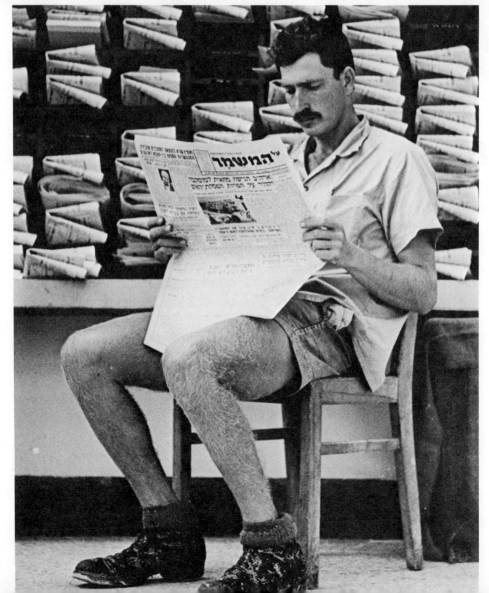

perhaps because they have lived so closely together while growing up.

When a couple decides to marry, they inform their parents and kibbutz authorities. A date is set and housing is arranged. A rabbi ("my master" in Hebrew, an ordained Jewish religious leader) conducts the ceremony in the traditional manner of Judaism. Israel's laws require that Jews be married in a religious ceremony. There are no civil marriages.

Often several couples are married at the same time. All the kibbutzniks dance and sing during the celebration that follows the ceremony.

A man and wife from different kibbutzim might spend six months at one kibbutz and six months at the other before deciding where to live. They might even decide to leave the kibbutz life and live in a city.

Should they stay on a kibbutz, the way of life there gives them much time to spend as they wish. When they are through with their daily job, there is little housework to do and most of the time they will not be involved in serving meals.

For entertainment, the kibbutz offers folk dancing, singing, plays, and lectures as well as movies. A kibbutznik's hobby can also be a means of entertainment for other kibbutz members. Kibbutz musicians, for example, present musical programs. The most popular musical instruments in Israel are the flute and the accordion.

The kibbutz life style encourages the development of leisure-time skills or hobbies. The freedom from the pressures of trying to "make it" in the business world or the professions is considered to be one of the greatest advantages of kibbutz living. The kibbutz approach toward work removes the tensions usually associated with earning a living. The kibbutz way of life gives an individual many hours which he may use as he pleases. As a result, many kibbutzniks become very skilled at their leisure occupations.

The kibbutzim also provide one or two-week vacations each year for members. Chaverim draw cash from the kibbutz treasury to pay for their trips. The vacation may be spent in one of the vacation facilities provided by the kibbutz federations. These facilities include apartments and restaurants in a resort on the Mediterranean coast of Israel.

Many kibbutzniks spend part of their leisure time in athletics. Soccer, volleyball, and basketball are the most popular sports. There is competition between teams on the same kibbutz. Kibbutz athletes also play teams from other kibbutzim. Non-playing kibbutzniks are lively fans at the games with other kibbutzim.

Israel has a variety of youth movements with units on the kibbutz. One of these groups, Maccabi Hatza'ir (Mah-kaa-BEE Ha-tza-EER, The Young Maccabee), emphasizes sports. Other youth movements are affiliated with Histadrut, scouting, political and religious groups, and the armed forces. The national sports organizations in Israel — Maccabi and Hapoel (Ha-POO-el) are the major ones — sponsor kibbutz athletic teams.

Many leisure-time activities for younger children and teenagers are organized through the youth groups. Hiking is a favorite kibbutz activity and frequent trips on foot are made into the hills and desert regions of Israel.

These hikes introduce young Israelis to what has been called "almost a national passion among the Israelis" — archaeology. This is the science of studying ancient history through materials long buried in the earth. It usually involves digging into the ground to discover things built and used by people who lived centuries ago. Many Israelis have a keen and knowledgeable interest in archaeology.

Sometimes, an unusual activity, such as keeping honey bees, will be undertaken by a kibbutznik. Many other chaverim find relaxation in doing something ordinary, such as working in a garden.

A few kibbutzim have outdoor swimming pools which are used for recreation for young and old as well as for competitive swimming.

Most kibbutzniks look to their ample leisure time as a means for either relaxing or doing something worthwhile yet satisfying. But on occasion a hobby can become a fulltime occupation — ceramics (making things from clay) or jewelry-making, for instance.

The kibbutz life style favors the development of creative persons such as artists, actors, musicians, and writers. The artist often displays his drawings, paintings, or sculpture in apartments or the dining hall. Sometimes he shows them at exhibitions in the cities. The kibbutz theater group might perform a play written by a member of the kibbutz. A composer's work might be presented by the orchestra on his kibbutz or by a regional orchestra formed by musicians from neighboring kibbutzim. One writer's interest might be poetry, another might work on the history of his kibbutz or edit the kibbutz newspaper.

However, free time on the kibbutz does not have to involve creative activity. It can be spent in well-supplied kibbutz libraries. Here there are books and magazines dealing with almost any subject. Many of these are in languages other than Hebrew because the chaverim have come to Israel from so many other countries.

But there is one book all these Jews know well — the Bible. The Jewish Bible (basically, the Christian Old Testament) is seen by many Israelis as a link between their new state and a 4,000-year-old culture. Although the majority of Israeli Jews do not practice their religion, they are deeply interested in the Bible as a history and as a guide to present-day problems in Israel. They study how the Jews of biblical times reacted in situations oftentimes similar to those faced today.

It is estimated that the nation's religious community includes less than one-fourth of the state's Jewish population, but Judaism is given special recognition and a privileged status by the government of Israel. Matters concerning births, marriages, divorces, burials, and the preparation and sale of food are, under Israeli law, regulated and observed by a council of rabbis.

Even so, four out of five Israelis ignore most of the 613 rules which a religious Jew is to observe. This attitude is also found on most kibbutzim. The religious kibbutz movement is the smallest of the national kibbutz federations. The religious federation's 4,000 members live on about a dozen kibbutzim where Jewish religious laws are followed. They observe Shabbat by holding religious services and emphasize the religious aspects of the Jewish holidays, all of which have biblical significance.

However, some kibbutzim which do not belong to the religious federation also have synagogues (SIN-ah-gogs, places where Jews worship — a house of prayer). And no one on any kibbutz is prohibited from practicing his religion, whether it be Judaism or another belief.

Shabbat is a special time on all kibbutzim, even those which observe it only as a day of rest from work or a day to spend with families.

Soldiers return home for Shabbat, holiday clothes are worn, Hebrew songs are sung, and the traditional lighting of candles takes place. The Friday evening meal is the most important meal of the week. The dining hall tables are covered with white table clothes and the meal is fancier than on other nights. There is a festive air on the kibbutz on Friday night.

Even on Shabbat, however, some chaverim must feed the livestock, see that the cows are milked, and provide the meals. All take their turn at chores that must be done on Shabbat, holidays, or other times when the entire kibbutz celebrates.

The Jewish holidays are observed as religious celebrations on some kibbutzim. The rest, however, emphasize the historical, agricultural, or national aspects of the holyday.

Passover, Purim (Poo-Rim), and Hanukkah (Cha-nuu-KAH, the feast of candles) are easily adapted to non-religious themes. Shavuoth (Sha-voo-OT) in the past included a brief reference to the first harvest but was centered on God's appearance on Mount Sinai to present Moses with the first five books of the Bible, the Torah. However on most kibbutzim it is the harvest theme that is emphasized, often with celebrations in the field. Festive clothes are worn and chaverim perform skits and participate in athletic contests with other kibbutzim.

Rosh Hashana (Rosh-Ha-sha-NAH) and Yom Kippur (Yom Kip-PUR) are two Jewish holidays that are difficult to observe without emphasizing religion. Rosh Hashana is the first day of the New Year according to the Hebrew calendar — 1971 is the year 5731 in this calendar. Yom Kippur ends the 10 days each fall, beginning with Rosh Hashana, which are dedicated to contrition for past misdeeds. It is the holiest day of the Jewish year.

Purim is a holiday in late winter which recalls the escape of the Jews from their Persian captors. The kibbutz children wear holiday costumes and traditional dances such as the hora provide an air of excitement on this holiday. The hora is the national dance of Israel. It is a folk dance dating from Southern Europe.

Passover recalls the exodus of Jews from slavery in Egypt about 3,300 years ago. This week-long observance can also be a celebration of freedom or a spring festival. Kibbutzniks spend the entire evening of the first day of Passover together. The Haggadah (Hah-gah-DA, "recitation" in Hebrew), the story of the escape from Egypt, is read at a communal sedar (SAY-dur, the ritual meal on this night). The sedar is an important event on the kibbutz. There is special food and drink and small pieces of matzah (MAHT-zah), the unleavened bread served during the sedar, are hidden early in the evening. Later the bread is found by the children who exchange it for prizes.

Many kibbutzim also celebrate the bar mitzvah (bar mits-VAH, "Son of the Commandment" in Hebrew). This is a traditional Jewish celebration marking a boy's 13th birthday. On religious kibbutzim, this is also the observance of a boy's becoming a man, therefore being permitted to participate in worship by reading a portion of the Torah. Bar mitzvah is more like a birthday party on non-religious kibbutzim.

Kibbutzniks also gather for messibot (meh-see-BOT, "parties" in Hebrew) on various occasions. These might be held to honor a youth group leaving to start their own kibbutz or to celebrate the move into a new dining hall.

Celebrating together, working together, living together, chaverim today have many opportunities for self-expression. The rural, usually peaceful, kibbutz setting provides the chaver a place to work, create, and, hopefully, to know what the Israeli hail and farewell bids him: Shalom — Peace.

YAIR SHAZAR, a sabra and a native kibbutznik, took the photographs used in this book. Photography has been this 31-year-old Israeli's avocation for the past eight years. His photos have appeared in prize-winning publications in Israel and in 1969 an exhibition was devoted to his pictures. Educated on the kibbutz, Shazar lives at Kibbutz Ein Hashofet with his wife and their daughter. Ein Hashofet was founded 34 years ago by American and Polish Jews. The name means "Spring of the Judge" in Hebrew. This kibbutz was named for the late United States Supreme Court Justice Louis Brandeis, one of the Zionists who provided support for the settlement. Ein Hashofet has grown from the 134 founding-members to 680 people today. This number includes 410 chaverim, 170 children, and 100 volunteers.

PAUL J. DEEGAN has written three other Amēcus Street books. A graduate of the University of Minnesota where he studied journalism and law, Deegan worked as a reporter and editor for several newspapers. Now living in suburban St. Paul, Minnesota, he and his wife, Dorothy, have three children, ages six to nine. The younger Deegans are unimpressed with the fact that kibbutz children seldom fight with one another.